LESSONS FROM THE TEACHER BUDDHA

LESSONS FROM

THE TEACHER

BUDDHA

by

Randy Bell

Published by
McKee Learning Foundation

ISBN-13:   978-0-9710549-7-4
ISBN-10:   0-9710549-7-5

Published by
        McKee Learning Foundation
        3215 Baltimore Branch Road
        Hot Springs, NC   28743

For more information, contact:

        Info@McKeeLearningFoundation.com

        www.McKeeLearningFoundation.com

TABLE OF CONTENTS

With Appreciation

to all those who have helped me
to understand and appreciate
the gift of the Buddha.

* * * * * * * * * * * * *

Cover Photo

*The Calm of the Buddha
in the Midst of Chaos*

Taken after a winter storm broke a tree that had been
previously struck by lightning,
leaving the Buddha statue and his essence
undisturbed among the resulting debris.

Randy Bell

LESSONS

FROM

THE

TEACHER

BUDDHA

I. PREFACE:

THE INTENTION

Lessons From The Teacher Buddha is the 2nd writing in the series of "Lessons" books. Following the same intention as with *Lessons From The Teacher Jesus*, this book looks to extract some of the core teachings from one of history's great master spiritual teachers, and to re-present those teachings to us in the language and context of today's modern life.

All of the great teaching masters, including Moses, Jesus, Buddha, Mohammed, Lao-Tzu, Confucius and others, were products of their time, geography, and local culture and audience. Each spoke in the terminology, shared experience, points of reference, and common vernacular of that setting. So also is done in this book: to present anew selected core truths of the Buddha not as regards substance, but as regards the time and vernacular relevant to today's western civilization audience. It is not just substituting modern words or expressions directly into familiar historical quotes, as has been often attempted of late with the Judaeo-Christian Bible. However well intended, this kind of jarring juxtaposition, neither fish nor fowl, always comes out feeling highly awkward, neither historical nor contemporary. This kind of forced approach often serves only to trivialize the passages and thereby frequently diminishes the impact of true meaning.

1

Throughout its history, Buddhism has purposefully and successfully adapted itself to local cultures, religions and the times as it has migrated across the world. For many, what is needed today is a new poetry, clear of meaning, faithful to the original message, yet spoken naturally in today's terminologies. It is in that same spirit of adaptation, of offering teachings of the Buddha to a new audience in a new time and place who might seek it out, that this book is purposed. It is a core of teachings relevant to all of us, teachings that transcend our particular religious history, practice, and dogmatic beliefs. I invite you to consider another possible roadmap as you follow your spiritual path.

"There are various kinds of assemblies, O Ānanda; assemblies of nobles, of Brahmans, of householders, of bhikkhus, and of other beings. When I used to enter an assembly, I always became, before I seated myself, in color like unto the color of my audience, and in voice like unto their voice. I spoke to them in their language and then with religious discourse, I instructed, quickened, and gladdened them."

The Buddha

II. <u>INTRODUCTION</u>

The Historical Buddha

The word Buddha is a general title, referring to one that has reached a certainly level of spiritual awareness described as "enlightenment." There have been many called a Buddha (an Enlightened or Awaken One) over time. However, the Buddha that occupies our attention was born @563 B.C.E. in northern India. His birth name was Siddhartha Gautama (or Siddhatta Gotama), born to a king of the Shakya clan of that region. He grew up within the riches and confines of his father, who provided him with all the comforts that money could buy, and who isolated him from the outside world and all of the suffering that was occurring there. Yet one day on a visit to the countryside, he saw four signs that he had not seen before: an old man; a man who was dying; a corpse; and a monk. From that moment he realized the existence of suffering in this world, and the role of a monk as his calling. At the age of 29 he made the decision to immediately leave his wife and young son, renounce his family ties and fortune, and join the ranks of the many ascetics then wandering the countryside who were seeking spiritual attainment. Yet after years of wandering in the practice of an ascetic life of denial, resulting in his near-death from self-deprivation, he concluded that such a life of extreme self-denial was not the path to overcoming suffering.

So Gautama decided upon a new course of action: unceasing meditation. He sat himself below a native bodhi tree, meditated for forty-nine days, and thereby attained complete enlightenment. He looked inside himself and saw his true nature, the true nature of earthly and human existence, and the cause of human suffering and its elimination. He thereby became a Buddha, known from this point on as the "historical

3

Buddha" or the Shakyamuni Buddha (*Sage of the Shakya Clan*).

After his previous ascetic companions realized his new state of being, these five prevailed upon him to teach them his method. The Buddha was a reluctant teacher. The difficulty of explaining his insights, experiences and transformation appeared daunting. Yet he realized, "there will be some who will understand." Thus began a forty year period of teaching by the Buddha across the Indian countryside, speaking to large crowds that turned out to hear him, embracing spiritual seekers who desired to become monks and nuns following in his footsteps, and establishing Buddhist centers for his followers. These activities and teachings formed the core basis for the Buddhism we know today. The Shakyamuni Buddha died @486 B.C.E.

These are the simple and basic facts of the Buddha's life. But such facts present only an incomplete picture of the man and his impact. It is the Message, the Method, and the Love of the Buddha that rise above the facts of his life. It is the picture of the man, one of quiet calm surrounded by an enveloping energy of love and acceptance. His egoless serenity profoundly affected those seekers who came into contact with him. All were accepted by him, and all were humbled and transformed by their experience with him. Absent of selfish ego and fear, he would carefully analyze and think through the questions presented to him, and guide one patiently to the personal conclusion which awaited discovery. Through this patient guiding, served up from a limitless love of all things and all beings, one's highest self could not help but be called forth and made whole.

It is his absolute clarity of thinking, coupled with a warm heart, and generously delivered with boundless unselfish compassion, that is the true essence of the Buddha.

The Work

The Buddha, then, came to see his ultimate role as that of a *teacher*. He was a master teacher, one of the few such great masters that have inhabited this world over time. Born into the Hindu faith of his native environment, he evolved from that background into an intellectual thought, a world-view and spiritual breadth previously unknown. He was always clear to his followers that Buddhism was about the method, the teachings, the understandings, not about him personally. He was fully resistant to any attempt at creating a cult status, to make him the focus and the centerpiece. He is not a divine figure, though miracles were attributed to him in the legends. He is not an intermediary to a divine existence or afterlife, or to a connection with a greater universal spirit. He is not an object of worship, but is one worthy of great respect and appreciation.

The Buddha simply taught his own method by which he had attained enlightenment, and what he had seen and experienced within that enlightenment. He believed that what he had discovered, what had worked for him, could also work for others. The Buddha made no special claims that his way was the *only* way to achieve a true spiritual outcome; it was more as "this worked for me; I will gladly share it with you as it may likely work for you also." In the end, the Buddha understood that enlightenment is a personal thing that must happen in a manner that works for that individual. Buddhism is therefore a *framework* within which each of us can pursue his/her own personal spiritual journey.

(The above was excerpted and adapted from my earlier book *Buddhism: An Introductory Guide*, to which the reader is referred for further background information on the Buddha and an overview of many fundamental Buddhist concepts.)

III. THE WRITTEN BUDDHA

The writings of the Buddha's teachings, along with some important talks by his primary disciple monks, are numerous to say the least. Like Jesus, even though both were educated men, neither wrote his teachings directly. The Buddha's teachings became part of an oral history, committed to memory by disciples and passed on by repetition to subsequent generations of followers. Only well after his death were the teachings – a series of talks, discourses and dialogs given as situations and opportunities presented themselves – ultimately transcribed to written form in a vast series of books (*sutras*).

The Buddha's teachings were not given in some orderly and structured manner to create some kind of Buddhist curriculum. They were given, and the resulting narratives were similarly written, as an occasion arose to teach on a particular discussion topic. They reflected on-going sermons, discussions, and responses to groups or individuals who came seeking out the Buddha's guidance and interpretations. Such seekers included kings and the very rich of his day; the itinerant and poor religious wanderers (of which there were many) from a variety of backgrounds zealously looking for fulfillment and spiritual realization; the monks and nuns who chose to follow the Buddha fulltime and, in so doing, thereby created the extensive Buddhist monastery network; and the everyday man or woman who sought a spiritual form of support and counsel as they lived their lives. All were welcomed by the Buddha and deemed eligible and capable of finding enlightenment and spiritual fulfillment, regardless of their position in life. Enlightenment is not reserved only for the monk and the nun.

Unlike Jesus, whose ministry covered the short span of only three years, the Buddha taught for over 40 years up until the day of his death. By benefit of time alone, this allowed for the creation of a vast body of teachings over a wide range of subject matter. From the Buddha, you will find extensive, multi-level, and in-depth teachings on such things as:

The Nature of Existence
- the meaning of earthly existence
- the role and impact that suffering plays in our lives, and how to eliminate to that suffering

Achieving Spiritual Fulfillment
- the Buddha's method by which he attained full enlightenment, which he shares with us
- the role and practice of meditation in seeking enlightenment
- how one should live a spiritual, ethical and enlightened life

Our Interactions
- our interrelationship with all things, both the sentient (things capable of feelings and perceptions) and the non-sentient
- the need for belonging to and honoring one's spiritual community (or "*sangha*")
- the role and expectations of the monk and the nun, at the various levels of spiritual attainment that they may achieve
- the role and expectations of the monk and the nun in maintaining the monastery

The Greater Realms That Surround Us
- the spiritual world that exists beyond that which we can see, touch, and know fully
- the cosmology and structure of that spiritual world

Sometimes the Buddha's teaching would be given in the form of a discourse, a teaching to his community of monks and nuns as like a homily or sermon. A poem might be used to

7

elevate the conversation to a more esthetic content. Other times, the Buddha's teaching would be a one-on-one question & answer dialog (as was favored by Socrates) on one particular topic raised by the questioner. The Buddha would then directly answer his questioner with the spiritual principle or concept relevant to the question asked. Sometimes he would ask the questioner to offer his/her own perspective or answer first in order to test the questioner's current spiritual maturity about the matter. Often, like Jesus, he would follow his reply (or answer the question itself) with a story, a parable, or an everyday illustration of how the question & answer might appear in an everyday circumstance. This would help to move the larger Spiritual Truth from an academic, conceptual discourse into a practical applied model that the listener could more readily apply to his/her own life. As intellectually sweeping as Buddhist philosophy is, the Buddha knew that concepts in the mind mean nothing until they are tested, applied, lived and confirmed on the field of the everyday. It is not enough to *know about* compassion; it is important to *live and experience* compassion every day in every circumstance.

The poetic style of the Buddha's teachings reflected its oral delivery format, supporting the intention for it to be remembered by all levels of educated listeners so that it could be learned, applied, repeated and passed on. These goals were typically supported in the texts by three key stylistic components:

- an almost sing-song like quality to the words and the phrasings, making the words almost musical and singable by listeners (songs are often easier to remember than speeches!)

- a presentation of examples of the *negative* aspect of the answer, followed then by examples of the *positive* aspect of the answer for clear contrast (i.e. see the different alternatives clearly, but choose the positive road)

- an enumeration of specific aspects and examples to a given concept (e.g. the 4 Noble Truths; the 8-Fold Path; the 5 Hindrances; the 4 Forms of Karma; the 3 Bases of Merit)

- constant repetition of the phrases (to reinforce the pointed ideas, and to more fully embed these ideas in the listener's memory)

In some respects, American traditional blues musicians will find the structure and style of these Buddhist teachings similar to their music, which is musically categorized as a "call and response" form.

A brief selected example of this poetic format could be:

> I do not perceive even one other thing, O monks, that is so unwieldy as an undeveloped mind. An undeveloped mind is truly unwieldy.
> I do not perceive even one other thing, O monks, that is so wieldy as an developed mind. A developed mind is truly wieldy.
> I do not perceive even one other thing, O monks, that leads to such great harm as an undeveloped mind. An undeveloped mind leads to great harm.
> I do not perceive even one other thing, O monks, that leads to such great benefit as a developed mind. A developed mind leads to great benefit.
> I do not perceive even one other thing, O monks, that when undeveloped and uncultivated entails such great suffering as the mind. The mind when undeveloped and uncultivated entails great suffering.
> I do not perceive even one other thing, O monks, that when developed and cultivated entails such great happiness as the mind. The mind when developed and cultivated entails great happiness.

Selected Teachings

In approaching the writing of this book, and given all the Buddha's writings that are available, it was easy to be overwhelmed in determining what lessons to include. I have therefore chosen to focus predominately on the Buddha's ethical and inter-relationship teachings, and the way he looks at how we should understand the life we have available to us. It is but a slice, but a key slice of that whole which he gives us to know.

And so, as I sat intently in a surrounding peaceful quiet, as I similarly asked of Jesus several years ago, I asked the Buddha, "Now, Buddha, speak directly to me those very same messages you spoke 2500 years ago, rephrased to this audience of one, and focusing on the *Lessons* to be learned from those teachings rather than the words and stories." So I make myself the Buddha's questioner, and sit and listen for his response. We engage in the dialog.

I humbly share with you the following responses.

THE

LESSONS

IV. <u>SPIRITUAL TRUTHS</u>

Lesson 1: There are three Treasures in your spiritual life that you should honor and give your utmost respect:

1. The spiritual Teacher(s), who has dedicated his/her life to your spiritual well-being.

2. The Teachings themselves, which serve to nourish and guide you on your spiritual path.

3. The Community of spiritual friends who you meet along the way, who share their presence and give you support in your journey, and you to them.

(from *The Three Treasures*)

Lesson 2: Find the universal Truths that exist. Focusing on your sense of self – your wants, desires, self-importance, pleasures, status – hides these Truths from your view. Lose that distorted focus and these Truths will open to you. In them, you will find true happiness, direction and fulfillment.

<u>Lesson 3</u>: Truth is available to all. There is no distinction between the monk who has taken religious vows, and the person living in the world with family. There are monks who fall because their heart is not pure and who belie their religious trappings. And there are humble householders whose goodness of heart takes them to the highest places.

Lesson 4: The spiritual pursuit towards Truth is never-ending. You progress from milestone to milestone. You do not arrive at your destination in one momentary flash. What you learn, you continually refine over time, constantly seeing more of the hidden aspects and broader meanings. You are never complacent in what you have learned thus far, but understand that more is always to be known. Knowledge is not of new things; it is deeper and fuller understandings of that which you have already seen. It is removing the outer layers to see the ultimate kernel of knowing that is in the core. That ever-expanding awareness is how knowledge moves to truth and wisdom.

Lesson 5: Humans beings are subject to the laws of cause and effect, like everything in nature. The present evolves from the past; the future is a product of the present. It is only by understanding the lessons you learn from your past that you can change your present and alter your future. Without such understanding and change, you exist in a constant unending pattern of repetition.

Lesson 6: Everything is transient. Nothing lasts forever. Birth and death, growth and decay, are immutable truths. Immortality exists only in your ability to change, adapt, and move within life and death as circumstances come to you. It is your heart that is forever, not your body nor the things with which you surround yourself.

Lesson 7: You live in constant change, as your external world is continually shifting around you. If you are overly attached to these external things, and use them to define who you are rather than living from your true inner self, then you fear such changes. But these changes are inevitable and unstoppable. Do not cling to what is. Be open to life as it comes; accept what comes and then release it. Doing so, you will move through life easily.

Lesson 8: We are all interdependent. You exist only in relationship to, and dependency upon, all other things. You have no existence solely on your own. You must therefore live in respect of that interdependency, and promote the good of all things living or otherwise. By your good deeds all will benefit.

<u>Lesson 9</u>: You see yourself, and your life around you, through the distorted lens of your own experiences. What you see is an illusion of your own making. You must see through this fog of illusion that clouds your understanding of things, and see the greater Truth that lies shrouded within. It is the *reality* of life with which you must properly interact, not the deluded life that you so often want to see.

Lesson 10: Undue focusing on the self leads to selfishness. Selfishness leads to wrongs, to evils, to those things that cause pain to yourself and to others. It is in Truth, seeing things as they truly are and living within that Truth, that you will find the peace of enlightenment, the happiness of contentment.

Lesson 11: Giving up your selfish emphasis, your focus on external accomplishment, is neither defeatist or resignation. It is freeing to be motivated by inner peace and confidence, unafraid of death, rather than being driven by momentary pleasures and accomplishments. But this Truth will remain hidden to those in the bondage of hate and desire, focused on the pursuits of this world. Worldly things fall away; the person inside you remains.

Lesson 12: Thinking leads to speech which leads to action. It all begins with thought. What you think *is* action. So let your thoughts be pure. Formulate them slowly, and ensure that they reflect your highest understandings and aspirations for yourself.

V. BIRTH, DEATH & REBIRTH

Lesson 13: Because you have been born, you are not free from aging and death. Aging and death are the inevitable result of being born.

Lesson 14: An outcast is not created by birth. One is outcast as a result of his/her bad actions. It is on this basis that one should be set aside, not by the circumstances of birth such as heritage, wealth, geography, beliefs.

<u>Lesson 15</u>: Some, by their birth, come into this world already in great standing and riches. Others arrive in a lower standing, lacking riches and struggling for survival each day. There are all manners of births in between those circumstances. But we are all conceived and born the same way, and at the end we will each die. No one is inherently greater or lesser than another by circumstance of birth. It is your actions that you choose and for which you are responsible that will make you inferior or superior. Our differences come only as a result of the life you choose to lead.

Lesson 16: We are all subject to old age, illness, and death, regardless of our station in life. Our evil acts will bring consequences to us throughout our lifetimes. So we should aspire to always do good in thought, speech and action.

Lesson 17: Your life is troubled, filled with pain, and brief. There is no way to avoid death. No way to prevent our own death or the death of others. No amount of grief can restore life. Remove your pain and suffering over death to restore peace in your life. Face the inevitability of your own death without fear, and be in peace with what you cannot prevent.

Lesson 18: Some persons after physical death will be reborn in misery, low standing and lesser forms. This new state will reflect a life not lived righteously. But for those who do live a righteous life, after death they will be reborn into a higher state in a heavenly destination.

(from *Karma and Rebirth*)

Lesson 19: When we are reborn, our new life reflects the prior life we chose to live. If we avoided killing, our reborn life will be long. If we avoided injuring others, our reborn life will be healthy. If we avoided being unpleasant, angry, bitter and hateful, our reborn life will attract others to us. If we avoided envy, our reborn life will attract respect from others. If we avoided stinginess, our reborn life will be rich. If we avoided arrogance, our reborn life will be honored. If we avoided spiritual indifference and laziness, our reborn life will be intelligent and wise.

<u>Lesson 20</u>: Those who die having eliminated envy and clinging from their life need not fear death. They will not be reborn into more suffering. Nothing will remain of them but their good thoughts, righteous acts, and the bliss that comes from having lived a life of truth and goodness. That is the ideal, and that is enough.

Lesson 21: Regardless of whatever outcomes may await you after death, live a life of good. Even if punishment does not happen to an evil one after death, you will still have been pure of heart. If an evil one is punished after death, you will have been spared such a fate. If there is no reward in heaven for a good life, you will still have lived a life of joy on this earth. And if there is another world reflecting a life of good deeds, you will most assuredly be found there. Living a good life today is right regardless of what awaits us after death.

(from *The Four Assurances*)

VI. THE SPIRITUAL PATH

<u>Lesson 22</u>: To find happiness in life, you must recognize Four

Truths that must guide your spiritual path:

1. There is sorrow in this world that we all experience.
2. Sorrow comes from desire, an insatiable wanting to have that which we do not have.
3. Sorrow can be eliminated by ending our clinging and attachment to that which we see as pleasurable.
4. Ending our sorrow is accomplished by living our lives within eight principles that lead to enlightened happiness (Noble Eightfold Path).

Living within these Truths, you will follow the right path.

(from *The 4 Noble Truths*)

Lesson 23: *Noble Eightfold Path – Right View*: Understand that sorrow is at the root of our existence. Seeing this cause, and eliminating craving as the cause of our suffering, will lead us to happiness. See the world as it truly is, not as we would have it to be or as we are told that it is.

(from the *Noble Eightfold Path*)

<u>Lesson 24</u>: *Noble Eightfold Path – Right Intention*: Be determined in pursuing the spiritual path defined by the Noble Eightfold Path. This will lead you to freedom and fulfillment through generosity to others, living ethically, replacing fear with faith and confidence in your future, and loving all others.

(from the *Noble Eightfold Path*)

<u>Lesson 25</u>: *Noble Eightfold Path – Right Speech*: Speak the truth always, factually as you know it in your mind. But select your words from the kindness of your heart. Spread no ill-will or gossip, which will only come back to cause ill-will towards you.

(from the *Noble Eightfold Path*)

Lesson 26: *Noble Eightfold Path – Right Action*: Ensure that your actions fulfill your words, that they be one and the same. Ensure that your actions promote unity, good and happiness rather than cause suffering in others. There are many routes to select from to get to where you are going; select thoughtfully.

(from the *Noble Eightfold Path*)

<u>Lesson 27</u>: *Noble Eightfold Path – Right Livelihood*: Avoid work that does not ennoble you and does not bring good to others. Specifically avoid trading in weapons, living beings, meat, liquors, and poisons. Accumulate wealth by hard work, earned by your own labors, performed ethically for a good greater than just for yourself.

(from the *Noble Eightfold Path*)

<u>Lesson 28</u>: *Noble Eightfold Path – Right Effort*: Make a deep commitment to follow your spiritual path, guided by these eightfold steps, undeterred by obstacles or frustrations.

(from the *Noble Eightfold Path*)

<u>Lesson 29</u>: *Noble Eightfold Path – Right Mindfulness*: Be constantly sensitive and aware of what is happening in this moment. Release the past, which we cannot change, to the past. Do not anticipate or project the future, which you cannot control. Live in this immediate present, which will be gone so very quickly.

(from the *Noble Eightfold Path*)

Lesson 30: *Noble Eightfold Path – Right Concentration*: Keep focused, calm, and do not waste energy. Do not be pulled back and forth by your pursuit of pleasure or avoidance of pain. Be clear in your thought and direction.

(*Noble Eightfold Path*)

Lesson 31: Do not enter the spiritual path for personal gain, or fame, or to achieve moral discipline or knowledge for its own sake. Rather, it is to free the mind from its entrapped state, and to live without fear and in full Truth, that you pursue the spiritual path.

Lesson 32: It matters not if you retreat into a spiritual sanctuary for your spiritual path, or stay active in everyday worldly activities, or whether you live in wealth or poverty. What matters is whether you have renounced selfishness, cleansed your heart, and committed to leading a righteous life. Live your life committed to quality, acting whole-heartedly in what you are called to do, without envy or hatred but residing in Truth.

Lesson 33: Be your own guide for your spiritual path. Take responsibility for your spiritual training, what you do, and how you do it. Hold fast to Truth, and seek fulfillment in the Truth. Look for those who can assist you, but rely on yourself and not on external help. The path has been shown to you. In the end, your spiritual attainment is your responsibility to do, not others to do for you.

Lesson 34: Following a spiritual path is not easy. In spite of your aspirations, many hurdles will arise along the way. You must constantly be on the lookout for the arising of sensual lust; for growing ill-will towards yourself or others; for drowsiness or dullness that weakens your attention; for a wandering mind or one filled with guilt over past events; or for the presence of doubt which can defeat your resolve. When you recognize these conditions arising, you must deepen your commitment and move through these hurdles even more renewed in order to continue to progress on your path.

(from *The Five Hindrances*)

<u>Lesson 35</u>: Let your spiritual beliefs not come from your traditions, family, ancestors, opinions, writings, reasoning, or a captivating spiritual teacher. All of these can help to inform you. But when you see all of these things in action, and you see good results flowing from them, such that in your own heart you *know* directly that these things are good – only then should you adopt such teachings as your own.

Lesson 36: Spend time in quiet prayer and meditation. Pray for the love and welfare of all beings, including your enemies. Pray for pity and compassion for those hurting and in distress. Pray for joy in reflecting upon the joy and prosperity of others. Pray for impurity, the impacts of wrong and evils, and how fleeting are the pleasures of the moment. And pray for serenity, rising above our everyday concerns, achieving calmness and perfect tranquility.

Lesson 37: When looking for your spiritual teacher, ask yourself: is that teacher without weakness of the spirit? Is that teacher without confusion in his/her thoughts? Has this teacher been consistently so over time, versus a recent convert? Has that teacher retained humility, avoiding the traps and excesses of fame? Does that teacher move without fear, impervious to the temptations so readily available? If yes, this is a teacher worthy of your respect and attention.

Lesson 38: When one finds a teacher, a teacher seen to be without greed, hate or delusion, then it is right to place your faith in that person and seek his/her counsel. From that basis of faith, respect flows for the teacher and the teachings; careful listening to the teachings follows; and the meanings of those teachings are accepted only after being thoughtfully considered carefully. Once accepted, those teachings create a desire in you for action, a striving to fulfill those teachings yourself. And from testing and experiencing those lessons, only then does wisdom come, and the ultimate knowing of the Truth.

Lesson 39: How do you know you are following the right path? Living uprightly by the Eightfold Noble Path is paramount, and you are alert to the lurking dangers in all that you should avoid. You train yourself to live a moral life, defined by holiness in word and deed. You sustain your life by pure means and right choices. You conduct yourself well, always mindful and aware of your thoughts and actions. Contentment and happiness mark your daily life.

Lesson 40: When you arrive at your spiritual destination and are fully enlightened about yourself and worldly existence, your mind is clear, always focused on the teachings, and filled with gladness regarding the understanding of these teachings. Calm in your body leads to happiness in your mind, in turn leading to full concentration of the mind – uncomplicated undistracted, clear, unperturbed by any surrounding chaos.

VII. <u>THE SPIRITUAL LIFE</u>

Lesson 41: Some seek spiritual accomplishment through the continuous pursuit of self-indulgent pleasure. Others seek a life of denial and sacrifice of their needs. Neither of these approaches is effective, and such extremes should be avoided. It is a balanced life that should be followed, avoiding extremes. Eat and drink as the body needs nourishment. Enjoy the pleasures that life offers to you without being dependent or a slave to them for your satisfactions.

(The Middle Way)

Lesson 42: One's outward form and presentation says nothing about what is in one's heart. Neither the poorly clad nor the richly ornamented necessarily have a claim on goodness. It is what is in one's spiritual heart, and the understanding of Truth, and the independence from worldly attachments, that speak to holiness.

Lesson 43: Your good and evil deeds follow you continually like shadows. What is most needed is a loving heart. Treat all deeds and people as if they were your own child. Do not mistreat others, but comfort and befriend those in need. Since it is impossible to escape the results of your deeds, choose to do good deeds.

Lesson 44: A truly holy person does not commit any unchaste act, takes no more than is given, and does not knowingly and maliciously take the life of any harmless creature. Having done these, do not boast of perfection, but retain your humility.

<u>Lesson 45</u>: All conditions of the heart that are not good, including unrighteous actions by deed, word or thought, must be burned away. Ego, lust, ill-will and delusion must be removed. Forbearance, love, charity and truth must be in your heart.

Lesson 46: The evils of the body are murder, theft, adultery.

The evils of the tongue are lying, slander, abuse, and idle talk.

The evils of the mind are envy, hatred, and misjudgment.

These evils are avoided by the spiritual person.

Lesson 47: Freedom from desire, hatred and illusion leads to good. Good is abstaining from killing, theft, and the pursuit of sensual pleasures; spreading falsehood and slander; letting go of envy; dismissing hatred; and being obedient to the Truth.

Lesson 48: Whatever you do, always act fully present in your mind to what is happening right now. Be thoughtful when you eat or drink. When you walk, stand, or sleep. When talking or being silent.

Lesson 49: As a dedicated monk: avoid taking what is not given; abstain from sexual relations and observe celibacy; do not engage in false speech; abstain from liquors; eat simply only one meal per day; do not engage in singing, dancing or dressing up in fancy attire; and avoid living in highly adorned and expensive places.

Lesson 50: The enlightened person will not be overly caught up in momentary events, Even while enjoying the pleasure or despairing the loss, it will be understood that these things will soon pass. Whether you experience gain or loss, fame or disrepute, praise or blame, or pleasure or pain, see these as only transitory moments. Stay in balance, not overly attached or dependent upon these moments.

Lesson 51: When you are hurt, you often seek to cover that hurt in pleasures to the senses to mask your pain. Done often, you become attached and dependent on such pleasures to mask what you are truly feeling. Do not attach yourself to such distractions. Recognize the hurts you have experienced, accept them for what they are, and move on with your life.

Lesson 52: People wish to live in peace. But too often they live in hate, reacting as enemies to each other. Such feelings come from envy, craving what others have, from wanting that which you do not have. Aspire to and work towards a good life. But be content with the life you have and what life brings you, rather than focusing on what you think is missing. Live simply with what is provided to you.

Lesson 53: Dedicate the wealth that you accumulate first to your family, co-workers and employees, and to friends. Set aside such a portion of that wealth as is necessary to provide for future unforeseen emergencies or losses. Share that wealth with those important in your life – family, friends, ancestors, the community and your god. Give support to those true spiritual beings and teachers who sustain your spirit on this earth.

Lesson 54: A kind person who uses wealth well will possess a great treasure. But one who hoards riches has no profit. Charity is rich in its returns, it is the greatest wealth. Holiness is better than ruling the whole world and owning all its riches. For when you die, no gold or treasures or possessions will follow you.

Lesson 55: The charitable person is loved by all, befriended by all, and rests peacefully at death. By giving away, we gain more, even if that gain is realized at a future time.

Lesson 56: A gift of minimal sacrifice made for personal gain is of little merit. But a gift of large sacrifice, made within love and with little expectation except for a greater good, is the best merit of all.

Lesson 57: When you give, give fully. Give out of faith. Give respectfully to the one who receives it. Give at the right time when it is needed. Give with a generous heart without bounds and without expectations of return. And give with respect for yourself and for that which you do.

VIII. <u>SPIRITUAL RELATIONSHIPS</u>

Lesson 58: Do not judge others without learning the facts of their actions. Whether condemning them or approving of them, either judgment is inappropriate if based upon ignorance. Only in factual truth can the judgment be right in both spirit and the law.

Lesson 59: He who deserves punishment must be punished, as it is his actions that caused his punishment, not his judge. But when the judge pronounces that judgment, let no malice or hatred be felt in effecting that punishment. Likewise, going to war to kill another is wrong. But one who goes to war after all efforts to try to preserve peace is not to blame, versus the one who caused the war. When victory is won, do not gloat or harbor ill-will. Make peace and be one again.

Lesson 60: We profess to be of great caring to things, ideas and people. But this caring is often a false emotion, a delusion of our unhealthy attachment to these very things. True caring is without attachment, without making things what we wish them to be. It is being un-entangled with them so that all beings are thereby free to be as they are.

Lesson 61: Being unattached to things does not mean that you do not care about them nor do you not interact with them. On the contrary, you should care very much about them. You care that such things are allowed to be just what they truly are, not what you would have them to be. And you do not cede the power to them to tell you how you will be, or think, or act. In such mutual freedom of love for what each thing is, each is able to fulfill and express exactly what their true inner nature is. You are unattached to outside things, but you are not uncaring, unconcerned, or unconnected with them.

Lesson 62: When people speak to you, it may be with one of several intentions: speaking truth or untruth; speaking timely or belatedly; speaking gently or harshly; speaking with an intention of good or bad towards you; or speaking in love or hate. Discern the intention of the speaker. Regardless of the speaker's intention, respond not in kind if you have been spoken to with bad intention. Always respond from your best intention and from an attitude of loving-kindness.

Lesson 63: If you are offered a present, and you decline it, then that present remains with the one who offered it. Similarly, if one insults or ridicules or abuses you, but you choose not to accept these in your heart and mind, then these things stay only with the abuser. Leave such ill-will with the one who would abuse you, and do not take it into yourself. Live only your own life, untroubled, and not another's version of you.

Lesson 64: When you may feel that someone has reviled, wronged or injured you, you may be tempted to create your own hatred for the wrong-doer. But hatred returned does not resolve hatred. The hatred we receive is only resolved by *not* hating in return. Do not live in someone else's shadow. Live your life as you know it to be right.

Lesson 65: Once you are victorious, embrace those who were once your enemy. Share your winnings, enhance their lives, give respect and welcome to them. Eliminate their need to hate you, to continue their fight with you. By such an embrace will all prosper and true peace be achieved.

Lesson 66: There are two people you can never fully repay by duty, attention or riches: your mother and your father. Your parents gave birth to you, fed you, raised you, and however perhaps well or poorly, prepared you for this life. For this they deserve your respect. If in some manner you can help them to see and live in spiritual truth – by this you will repay them in full.

Lesson 67: There are four kinds of marriages: one in which he of poor heart lives with her of poor heart; he of poor heart lives with her of pure heart; he of pure heart lives with her of poor heart; and he of pure heart lives with her of pure heart. Living pure of heart means avoiding the destruction of life, abstaining from liquor, being of good character, being free of stinginess, and respecting the virtues. This is the kind of relationship to aspire to: sharing the same faith, morality, generosity of spirit, and wisdom.

IX. <u>SPIRITUAL COMMUNITY</u>

Lesson 68: One who attempts to follow a spiritual path alone risks falling back into his/her old ways. Surround yourself with those who can strengthen your resolve, demonstrate your aspirations, assist you with guidance, and support your journey. Such is a holy community that supports your faith.

Lesson 69: To build the love and respect of others in your community, always be in loving-kindness in your thoughts, in your words, in your actions. Find those things you have in common with others. Be focused on this commonality with them rather than your differences. Share with them that which you have been fortunate enough to receive.

Lesson 70: Surround yourself with those righteous and wise ones who inspire you and encourage your righteous path. Do not surround yourself with the foolish, the selfish, the quarrelsome. Let them pass and walk on their own.

Lesson 71: Be merciful to those who struggle, and have compassion on them. Pity those hopelessly entangled in sorrow. Help those who are almost free from worldliness to open the door of true immortality.

Lesson 72: How does a layperson achieve spiritual fulfillment and find happiness within the family, if you choose not to adopt the solitary life of the monk? By being skillful, honest and organized in your profession. By protecting for the benefit of your family the honest wealth that you accumulate. By befriending people of good character, faith and virtue who are worthy of your emulation. By keeping your life in proper balance, living neither extravagantly nor poorly so as to ensure the proper welfare of your family. You achieve spiritual fulfillment and find happiness by living a moral life in faith, generous to those around you, guided by the wisdom of the Truth.

X. <u>CONCLUSION: THE BUDDHA</u>

Lesson 73: The role of the Buddha is to be honored, not worshiped. The Buddha is he who originated this spiritual path previously unknown. He knows this path, is skilled in this path, and he has been kind enough to share it with you. By so doing, he allows you to similarly know it. It is for this that you honor him.

Lesson 74: The Teachings from the Buddha:

"My doctrine is pure and it makes no discrimination between the noble and ignoble, rich and poor.

My doctrine is like unto water which cleanses all without distinction.

My doctrine is like unto fire which consumes all things that exist between heaven and earth, great and small.

My doctrine is like unto the heavens, for there is room in it, ample room for the reception of all, for men and women, boys and girls, the powerful and the lowly."

(Poem by the Buddha)

<u>Lesson 75</u>: Blessing by the Buddha.

May every creature abound in well-being and peace.
May every living being, weak or strong, the long and the
    small,
The short and the medium-sized, the mean and the great,
May every living being, seen or unseen, those dwelling far off,
Those near by, those already born, those waiting to be born,

May all attain inward peace.
Let no one deceive another.
Let no one despise another in any situation.
Let no one, from antipathy or hatred, wish evil to anyone at
    all.
Just as a mother, with her own life, protects her only son from
    hurt,
So within yourself foster a limitless concern for every living
    creature.

Display a heart of boundless love for all the world,
In all its height and depth and broad extent.
Love unrestrained, without hate or enmity.
Then as you stand or walk, sit or lie, until overcome by
    drowsiness,
Devote your mind entirely to this.
It is known as living here life divine.

(H.H. 14th Dalai Lama)

"Peace does not mean to be in a place where there is no noise, trouble or hard work. It means to be in the midst of these things and still be calm in your heart."

(unknown)

PUBLICATIONS LIST

Other publications by Randy Bell available from McKee
Learning Foundation:

www.McKeeLearningFoundation.com

Executive's Guidebook for Institutional Change
ISBN 0-9710549-0-8

Buddhism: An Introductory Guide
ISBN-13   978-0-9710549-1-2

Lessons from the Teacher Jesus
ISBN-13:   978-0-9710549-2-9

Lessons from the Teacher Jesus- The Teachings   (pocket
edition)
ISBN-13:   978-0-9710549-3-6

Career Choices For Your Soul
ISBN-13:   978-0-9710549-4-3

God and Me: A Statement of Belief
ISBN-13:   978-0-9710549-5-0

Forms of Meditation: Methods and Practices for
Contemplation and Prayer
ISBN-13:   978-0-9710549-6-7